—The Ultimate—
BAGEL
Cookbook

—The Ultimate—
BAGEL
Cookbook

BY

SARAH MAXWELL

APPLE

A QUINTET BOOK

Published by The Apple Press
6 Blundell Street
London N7 9BH

ISBN 1–85076–594–4

This book was designed and produced by
Quintet Publishing Limited
6 Blundell Street
London N7 9BH

Creative Director: Richard Dewing
Designer: Isobel Gillan
Senior Editor: Laura Sandelson
Editor: Barbara Croxford
Photographer: Tim Hill
Home Economist and Stylist: Sarah Maxwell

Typeset in Great Britain by
Central Southern Typesetters, Eastbourne
Manufactured in Hong Kong by Regent Publishing Services Ltd.
Printed in China by Leefung-Asco Printers Ltd.

Author Acknowledgements
With special thanks to my grandma and poppa, Norma, Lok Zen and, as
always, Jenny, Paul and Oliver whose love, help and support make it all
worthwhile.

CONTENTS

INTRODUCTION

★ ★ ★ ★ ★

You say Bagel, I say Beigel . . . basically depends on whether you are of Polish or Russian origin. At the end of the day, we all know we are talking about the one and only bread roll of its kind – unique in taste, texture and method of cooking. Being the only type of bread that is boiled before it is baked, gives the bagel that distinguishable crispiness on the outside and delectable chewiness on the inside.

Whilst bakers compete vigorously to create the most authentic bagel, the customer is in hot pursuit of the most scrumptious and original bagel filling. *The Bagel Book* is positively oozing with delicious fillings for bagels, ranging from the more classic to the very exotic, from the totally meatless to the sweet temptations in the last chapter.

Quantities are given to serve small numbers on the basis that bagels satisfy an instant craving, a spontaneous desire when there is only you and perhaps one other person around at the same time with the same addiction. Other recipes cater for large numbers; but whatever the recipe, you only need to increase or reduce the quantities of ingredients to fill more or fewer bagels.

The essence of this book is light-hearted and fun, offering plenty of delicious ideas for bagel fillings. Choose your favourite bagel, such as sesame or poppy seed, onion or plain, to go with your favourite filling. Go crazy and experiment. These recipes can be used for ideas which you can adapt and change to suit your own personal tastes and desires.

STORING BAGELS

There is no doubt that bagels are best eaten fresh on the day they are made. However, day old bagels can be warmed in the oven or cut in half and toasted. They can also be frozen in airtight bags or containers for up to 3 months. These will need to be warmed in the oven from frozen, or toasted before filling and serving.

ABOVE Black Forest Bagel (see page 90)

LEFT Bagels are round, boiled rolls with a hole in the middle, symbolizing the continuous circle of life.

BASIC BAGELS

★ ★ ★

This recipe makes about sixteen bagels of average size. If you prefer your bagels slightly bigger or smaller than average, then you can make them to suit your preference. Bear in mind, the bigger they are the fewer bagels you will make and vice versa.

MAKES ABOUT 16 BAGELS

225 ml/8 fl oz boiling milk

50 g/2 oz butter, plus extra for greasing

25 g/1 oz caster sugar

15 g/½ oz fresh yeast or 2 tsp dried

pinch of salt

1 egg, separated

400 g/14 oz strong plain flour

30 ml/2 tbsp milk

METHOD

Pour the boiling milk into a mixing bowl and stir in the butter and sugar. Leave the mixture to stand until lukewarm.

Sprinkle over the yeast and leave to stand in a warm place for about 5 minutes for fresh yeast and about 15 minutes for dried, until the mixture is frothy.

Stir the salt and egg white into the yeast mixture, then gradually beat in the flour to make a soft dough. Turn the dough onto a lightly floured surface and knead for about 5 minutes, until smooth and elastic.

Return the dough to the cleaned bowl and cover with cling wrap. Leave in a warm place to rise for about 1 hour, or until doubled in size.

Turn the risen dough out onto the work surface and knock back to its original size. Divide the dough into sixteen even-sized pieces.

Roll a piece of dough into a "sausage" shape, then wrap it round your fingers on one hand to make a "hoop" shape. Pinch the join together firmly and repeat with the other pieces of dough.

Place the bagels on greased baking sheets covered with greased greaseproof paper. Leave enough space between them so they can rise without touching, then cover loosely with a sheet of cling wrap. Return the bagels to a warm place to prove for about 10 minutes.

Preheat the oven to 200°C/400°F/Gas Mark 6. Bring a large saucepan of water to the boil, then reduce the heat and simmer. Gently drop the bagels into the water, only a few at a time to prevent them touching.

Simmer the bagels for about 15–20 seconds, or until puffy and beginning to swell. Using a slotted spoon, lift the bagels out of the water and return to the baking sheets. Repeat the process with the remaining bagels.

Mix together the egg yolk and milk in a small bowl. Lightly brush the bagels evenly with the egg glaze. Bake for about 20 minutes, or until risen, golden and hollow sounding when tapped. Transfer to a wire rack to cool.

VARIATIONS

★ ★ ★

POPPY SEED BAGELS
Sprinkle the bagels generously with poppy seeds after they have been glazed.

ONION BAGELS
Heat 45 ml/3 tbsp vegetable oil in a large frying pan and add 2 large finely chopped onions. Cook for about 10 minutes or until golden brown. Drain. Place a little of the fried onion on the top of the bagels after they have been glazed.

SESAME SEED BAGELS
Sprinkle the bagels generously with sesame seeds after they have been glazed.

CINNAMON AND RAISIN BAGELS
Substitute 150 g/5 oz of the strong plain flour with wholewheat flour and add 100 g/4 oz raisins and 1 tbsp ground cinnamon to the dry ingredients. Stir well and continue following the recipe.

BAGEL CHIPS

★ ★ ★ ★ ★

A perfect anytime snack made with day-old bagels. Use your imagination when it comes to your own favourite flavourings, but you'll have a hard job beating the great taste of this recipe.

SERVES 4–6

2 onion bagels

sunflower oil, for shallow frying

2 cloves of garlic, crushed

pinch of dried mixed herbs

salt and freshly ground black pepper

3–4 tbsp freshly grated Parmesan cheese

METHOD

Cut the bagels into small, bite-size pieces.

Heat the oil in a frying pan and add the garlic and mixed herbs. Cook for about 1 minute. Add the bagel pieces in batches, turning them for about 3–5 minutes, or until golden brown and crisp.

Drain the bagel chips on absorbent kitchen paper. Serve in a warm serving dish, seasoned with salt and pepper and sprinkled with freshly grated Parmesan cheese.

11

CLASSIC
BAGELS

★ ★ ★ ★ ★

SUNDAY BEST

★ ★ ★ ★ ★

Make use of the leftover joint in this delicious bagel filling.

SERVES 2

2 onion bagels

butter or margarine, for spreading

100 g/4 oz chilled roast beef, thinly sliced

2 tomatoes, thinly sliced

15–20 ml/3–4 tbsp horseradish sauce

salt and freshly ground black pepper

METHOD

Cut the bagels in half horizontally and lightly butter the cut surfaces.

Pile the sliced beef onto the base of each bagel, then top with slices of fresh tomato.

Spread over a little horseradish. Season with salt and freshly ground black pepper, before putting on the lid.

TOWER OF BAGEL

★ ★ ★ ★ ★

Not one, but two delicious layers of smooth, soft creamy cheese topped with smoked salmon.

SERVES 2

2 sesame bagels

butter or margarine, for spreading

75 g/3 oz cream (full-fat soft) cheese

75 g/3 oz smoked salmon, sliced wafer thin

tiny fresh dill sprigs

½ lemon, for squeezing

freshly ground black pepper

capers and baby gherkins, to serve

METHOD

Using a large serrated knife, slice the bagels into three layers. Butter the bottom layer and top surface of the middle layer sparingly.

Spread a generous layer of cream cheese on top of the buttered layers. Top with sliced smoked salmon, cutting and folding it to fit the bagel.

Scatter a few tiny sprigs of fresh dill over the smoked salmon and sprinkle with a squeeze of lemon juice. Grind some freshly ground black pepper over the top and layer up the bagel, finishing with the sesame coated lid. Serve with capers and gherkins.

Tower of Bagel

BROOKLYN BAGEL

★ ★ ★ ★ ★

*Salt beef is at its best when fresh, moist, warm and crumbly. Piled
into a soft, chewy bagel with all the trimmings,
it's unbeatable!*

SERVES 2

2 poppy seed bagels

butter or margarine, for spreading

American mustard

175 g/6 oz warm fresh salt beef, sliced

50 g/2 oz cooked beetroot, sliced

2 small pickled cucumbers

silverskin cocktail onions and fresh flat parsley sprigs, to garnish

METHOD

Cut the bagels in half horizontally and lightly butter
the cut surfaces.

Spread a thin layer of mustard on the base of each
bagel and pile the sliced salt beef on top. Add a little
more mustard, if you like it hot, then add a layer of
beetroot, then sliced pickled cucumber.

Place the bagel lids on top and serve with cocktail
onions and parsley sprigs.

FRIDAY NIGHT BAGEL

★ ★ ★ ★

Chopped liver is a Jewish delicacy, available from Jewish delicatessens and major supermarkets, and usually served at the Sabbath on Friday nights.

SERVES 2

2 plain or caraway bagels

butter or margarine, for spreading

75 g/3 oz chopped liver

1 hard-boiled egg

chopped fresh parsley, to garnish

lettuce leaves and baby gherkins, to serve

METHOD

Cut the bagels in half horizontally and lightly butter the cut surfaces.

Generously pile the chopped liver on the base of each bagel. Spread out evenly and make line indentations with the knife.

Separate the yolk from the white of the egg. Press separately through a sieve onto a small plate. Use the sieved white and yolk of the egg to fill the channels in the chopped liver, making lines across the surface.

Sprinkle with chopped parsley and top with the bagel lid. Serve with a little lettuce and baby gherkins.

THE BIG DIPPER

★ ★ ★ ★ ★

*For dieting bagel-lovers everywhere, this one's for you. Piles of cool,
fresh cottage cheese, served with a slice of juicy pineapple and
topped with crisp cubes of cucumber.*

SERVES 2

1 bagel

50 g/2 oz cottage cheese

mustard and cress

2 slices of canned pineapple in fruit juice, drained

10 cm/4 in piece of cucumber, finely diced

salt and freshly ground black pepper

yellow pickled onions and fresh dill sprigs, to serve

METHOD

Cut the bagel in half horizontally and place each half
on an individual plate.

Divide the cottage cheese between the bagel
halves and spread out evenly. Arrange a layer of
mustard and cress in a circle on top.

Place a slice of pineapple on top of the mustard
and cress, then pile half the diced cucumber in the
centre of each. Season with salt and black pepper.
Serve with yellow pickled onions and dill sprigs.

BENEDICT BAGEL

★ ★ ★ ★ ★

*The combination of the melted cheese and soft poached egg
dripping in the subtle taste of hollandaise sauce makes this melt-in-
the-mouth bagel a perfect breakfast or lunchtime snack.*

SERVES 2

2 bagels

50 g/2 oz Cheddar cheese, thinly sliced

2 eggs

a little butter or margarine

60 ml/4 tbsp hollandaise sauce

chopped fresh parsley and parsley sprigs, to garnish

METHOD

Slice the tops off the bagels and toast the bases. Leave the bagels on the grill pan and top with the sliced cheese.

Poach the eggs in a little butter until they are cooked the way you like them.

Just before the end of the cooking time, place the cheese topped bagels under a hot grill to melt. Place the bagel bases on individual serving plates and top each with a poached egg.

Drizzle on the hollandaise sauce and sprinkle over the chopped parsley. Replace the bagel "lids". Garnish with the parsley sprigs and serve immediately.

DELI SPECIAL BAGEL

★ ★ ★ ★ ★

Some like it hot! Packed full of succulent salamis and peppery pickles, this bagel will certainly liven up your palate!

SERVES 2

2 poppy seed bagels

butter or margarine, for spreading

2 tbsp piccalilli pickle

50 g/2 oz pastrami

25 g/1 oz beef salami

American mustard

pickled chillies, to serve

METHOD

Cut the bagels horizontally into three even layers and lightly spread with butter.

Spread the piccalilli pickle over the bottom layers. Pile the pastrami on top of the piccalilli, then put on the middle bagel layers.

Arrange the beef salami on top and add enough mustard to suit your taste. Put the bagel lids on and serve with pickled chillies.

Deli Special Bagel

BROADWAY BAGEL

★ ★ ★ ★ ★

A classic breakfast bagel in America – filled with hash browns and a fried egg!

SERVES 2

1 small onion, finely chopped

1 large potato, peeled and grated

pinch of dried thyme

salt and freshly ground black pepper

50 g/2 oz butter or margarine, plus extra for spreading

2 eggs

2 bagels

METHOD

In a mixing bowl, combine the onion, potato, dried thyme and salt and black pepper. Mix well.

Melt a little more than half of the butter in a large non-stick frying pan and add the potato mixture. Flatten it out in the pan and cook for about 10 minutes.

Turn the hash browns over, don't worry if they break up, and continue to cook for about 5–10 minutes until golden. Just before the end of the cooking time, melt the remaining butter in another frying pan and fry the eggs, turning them over, if you like.

Cut the bagels in half horizontally and toast. Lightly butter the cut surfaces, then put the bases on individual plates.

Pile on the hash browns, then put an egg on top. Season again with salt and freshly ground black pepper, then serve with the bagel lids.

ITALIAN BAGEL

★ ★ ★ ★ ★

*This is a mouth-watering combination of some of the finest Italian ingredients.
Where better to combine them than inside a warm, fresh bagel?*

SERVES 2

2 sesame seed bagels

a little extra virgin olive oil

25 g/1 oz Milano salami, very thinly sliced

50 g/2 oz mozzarella cheese, sliced

2 tomatoes, sliced

fresh basil leaves, torn

salt and freshly ground black pepper

mayonnaise, to taste

black and green Italian olives, to serve

METHOD

Cut the bagels in half horizontally and lightly brush the cut surfaces with a little olive oil.

Arrange the salami on the base of each bagel, then place a layer of Mozzarella cheese on top.

Divide the tomato slices and the torn basil leaves between the bagels, then season with salt and freshly ground black pepper.

Spoon over some mayonnaise, then top with the bagel lids. Cut in half and serve with Italian olives.

HERRING LOVER'S BAGEL

★ ★ ★ ★ ★

If you like herring, then this creamy herring topped bagel
is for you.

SERVES 2

1 bagel

butter or margarine, for spreading

100 g/4 oz jar skinned pickled herring fillets with onion

45 ml/3 tbsp single cream

freshly ground black pepper

1 tbsp chopped fresh dill

lemon wedges and fresh dill sprigs, to garnish

METHOD

Cut the bagel in half horizontally and toast on both sides. Lightly butter the cut surfaces.

In a small bowl combine the herring fillets, cream, freshly ground black pepper and chopped dill. Stir to coat the fish in the sauce.

Pile the herring mixture onto the bagel halves. Serve garnished with lemon wedges and fresh dill sprigs.

HOT TUNA BAGEL

★ ★ ★ ★ ★

A delicious combination of tender pieces of tuna and crunchy sweet peppers.

SERVES 2

2 sesame seed bagels

butter or margarine, for spreading

few leaves of Little Gem lettuce, washed

200 g/7 oz can tuna chunks in vegetable oil, drained

½ orange pepper, seeded and finely diced

½ green pepper, seeded and finely diced

1 small onion, very finely chopped

45–60 ml/3–4 tbsp mayonnaise, plus extra for drizzling

juice of ½ lemon

salt and freshly ground black pepper

½ tsp chilli powder

½ tsp ground turmeric

fresh dill sprigs, to garnish

METHOD

Cut the bagels in half horizontally and lightly spread the cut surfaces with butter. Place the top halves upside down on serving plates and arrange a few of the lettuce leaves on top.

In a mixing bowl, combine the tuna, diced peppers, onion, mayonnaise and lemon juice and season with salt and black pepper. Stir gently to mix.

Divide the tuna mixture between the bagels, reserving about two tablespoons in the bowl. Top with the other half of each bagel. Shred the remaining lettuce and arrange on top of each bagel. Spoon over the remaining tuna mixture and drizzle over extra mayonnaise.

Sprinkle over the chilli powder and ground turmeric. Garnish each with a sprig of fresh dill.

CLUB CLASS BAGEL

★ ★ ★ ★ ★

A first class bagel, made with only the finest ingredients.

SERVES 2

2 poppy seed bagels

butter or margarine, for spreading

a few lettuce leaves, washed

75 g/3 oz wafer thin pastrami

1 tomato, thinly sliced

75 g/3 oz wafer thin chicken or turkey breast

2 tbsp American or English mustard

salt and freshly ground black pepper

METHOD

Cut the bagels horizontally into three even layers and lightly butter. Tear the lettuce leaves into pieces and arrange on the bottom layer of each bagel.

Pile the pastrami on top of the lettuce, then position the middle layer of bagel. Arrange the tomato slices, then a single layer of wafer thin chicken or turkey on top.

Spoon over the mustard, then add the remaining chicken or turkey. Season with salt and freshly ground black pepper. Place the bagel lids on top and serve.

BAGEL-BURGER

★ ★ ★ ★ ★

This double burger bagel is a complete meal in itself. Forget the fries, who needs them?

SERVES 2

2 sesame seed bagels

4 × 100 g/4 oz beef burgers

few crisp lettuce leaves, washed

1 tomato, thinly sliced

2 slices Cheddar cheese

60 ml/4 tbsp tomato ketchup

30 ml/2 tbsp mayonnaise

fresh parsley sprigs, to garnish

METHOD

Cut the bagels in half horizontally and set aside. Fry the burgers until cooked to your taste. Place a few lettuce leaves on the base of each bagel and top with tomato slices.

About a minute before the burgers are cooked, place a slice of cheese on top of two of them and cook until just melting. Place the cheese topped burgers on top of the tomato layer of each bagel and top with a little ketchup.

Position the other burger on top and add a little more ketchup with some mayonnaise. Put on the bagel lid and serve on a few lettuce leaves, garnished with fresh parsley sprigs.

DOUBLE CHEESE MELT

★ ★ ★ ★ ★

This is no ordinary cheese sandwich! The layers of delicately flavoured cheese, salad and dressing create a bagel to savour as it melts in your mouth.

SERVES 2

2 bagels

butter or margarine, for spreading

75 g/3 oz Jarlsberg cheese, grated

75 g/3 oz red Leicester cheese, grated

30 ml/2 tbsp mayonnaise

10 ml/2 tsp French dressing

salt and freshly ground black pepper

1 tomato, sliced

few leaves of crisp lettuce, shredded

pickles, to serve

METHOD

Cut the bagels horizontally into three even layers and lightly butter them.

Divide the Jarlsberg cheese between the two bottom layers and the red Leicester cheese between the two middle layers. Lightly grill the cheese layers, until just melting.

In a small bowl mix together the mayonnaise and French dressing and season with salt and freshly ground black pepper.

Arrange the sliced tomato on top of the Jarlsberg and drizzle over a little of the dressing mixture. Place the red Leicester layer on top.

Divide the lettuce between the bagels and drizzle over a little more dressing. Put the bagel lids on and serve immediately with a few pickles.

Bagel-Burger

GRANDMA'S SPECIAL

★ ★ ★ ★ ★

A classic in any traditional Jewish household – just like Grandma used to make.

SERVES 2

3 hard-boiled eggs, shelled and chopped

6 tbsp chopped spring onion tops

60 ml/4 tbsp mayonnaise

salt and freshly ground black pepper

2 sesame seed bagels

butter or margarine, for spreading

1 tbsp chopped fresh parsley

pickled cucumbers, to serve

METHOD

First make the egg and onion mixture. Place the chopped egg, spring onion tops, mayonnaise and salt and freshly ground black pepper in a bowl and mix until evenly combined.

Cut the bagels in half horizontally and butter the cut surfaces. Divide the egg and onion mixture between the base of each bagel and sprinkle over the chopped parsley. Top with the bagel lids.

Serve cut in half crossways with pickled cucumbers.

SWISS CHEESE BAGEL

★ ★ ★ ★ ★

*You will savour every bite of this freshly baked onion bagel, packed
full of wafer thin slices of subtle tasting Swiss cheese.*

SERVES 2

2 onion bagels

butter or margarine, for spreading

½ ripe avocado, sliced

few drops of freshly squeezed lemon juice

75 g/3 oz Emmental cheese, thinly sliced

salt and freshly ground black pepper

fresh flat leaf parsley sprigs, to garnish

METHOD

Cut the bagels in half horizontally and lightly butter the cut surfaces.

Divide the sliced avocado between the bases of the bagels and sprinkle over a few drops of lemon juice.

Pile the Emmental cheese on top of the avocado and season with salt and freshly ground black pepper. Put on the bagel lids and garnish with sprigs of fresh parsley.

BIG BANG BAGEL

★ ★ ★ ★ ★

One of the more complicated fillings, but well worth the effort.

SERVES 4

30 ml/2 tbsp olive oil

1 small onion, finely chopped

1 clove of garlic, crushed

450 g/1 lb minced steak

30 ml/2 tbsp tomato purée

200 g/7 oz can red kidney beans, drained

225 ml/8 fl oz stock

1 tbsp flour

1–2 tbsp chilli powder

pinch of dried oregano

salt and freshly ground black pepper

2 bagels

60 ml/4 tbsp sour cream

2 tbsp snipped fresh chives

METHOD

First make the chilli. Heat the oil in a saucepan and add the onion and garlic. Cook for about 5 minutes, then stir in the steak. Cook, stirring frequently, for about 10 minutes, then add the tomato purée, kidney beans and stock.

Mix the flour and chilli powder together in a small bowl with a little water to make a smooth paste. Stir into the meat mixture with the oregano and season with salt and freshly ground black pepper. Simmer the chilli for about 1 hour, stirring occasionally.

Cut the bagels in half horizontally and place each half on a separate serving plate. Spoon the chilli on top of the bagel halves and top with sour cream and chives. Serve immediately.

PINK CADILLAC

★ ★ ★ ★ ★

An interesting layered bagel filled with salmon, salad and mayonnaise.

SERVES 2

1 large sesame seed bagel

butter or margarine, for spreading

15 cm/6 in piece of cucumber, grated

200 g/7 oz can pink salmon in vegetable oil, drained

¼ red pepper, seeded and very finely diced

30–45 ml/2–3 tbsp mayonnaise

squeeze of fresh lemon juice

salt and freshly ground black pepper

fresh dill sprigs, lemon and lime slices, to garnish

METHOD

Thinly cut the bagel horizontally into five even slices and lightly butter.

Lay the bagel slices out on a work surface. Except for the lid, divide the grated cucumber between the layers.

To make the salmon filling, place the salmon in a bowl and add the diced pepper, mayonnaise, lemon juice and salt and freshly ground black pepper. Stir to mix.

Divide the salmon mixture between the bagel slices, then sprinkle a few tiny dill sprigs over each layer. Pile up on a serving plate, finishing with the lid. Serve garnished with fresh dill sprigs and lemon and lime slices.

Pink Cadillac

BAGEL PARMESAN

★ ★ ★ ★ ★

*A definite Mediterranean-style bagel – warm and garlicky. This one
makes a delicious starter or snack.*

SERVES 4

2 bagels

2 cloves of garlic, quartered

60 ml/4 tbsp extra virgin olive oil

400 g/14 oz can artichoke hearts, drained and quartered

100 g/4 oz antipasto with carrots and olives in oil, drained

3–4 tbsp chopped spring onion tops

75 g/3 oz freshly grated Parmesan cheese

freshly ground black pepper

fresh flat leaf parsley sprigs, to garnish

METHOD

Cut the bagels in half horizontally and toast the cut
surfaces. Put the garlic in a small jug and add the olive
oil. Stir and set aside.

Arrange the artichoke pieces on the toasted bagel
halves and scatter over some of the antipasto and the
spring onion tops. Sprinkle over the Parmesan cheese
and ground black pepper, then generously drizzle over
the garlic oil.

Grill the bagels again for 2–3 minutes, just to melt
the cheese slightly. Serve immediately on individual
serving plates, garnished with the reserved antipasto
and sprigs of fresh flat leaf parsley.

CALIFORNIA DREAM

★ ★ ★ ★ ★

*Healthy, crisp and crunchy, this bagel makes the perfect
light lunch snack.*

SERVES 2

2 plain bagels

butter or margarine, for spreading

1 red apple, cored and chopped

1 stick of celery, sliced

25 g/1 oz sultanas

25 g/1 oz peanuts, shelled

30–45 ml/2–3 tbsp mayonnaise

salt and freshly ground black pepper

1 tbsp chopped flat leaf parsley

flat leaf parsley sprig, to garnish

METHOD

Cut the bagels in half horizontally and lightly butter
the surfaces. Cut the top halves into quarters.

To make the filling: in a mixing bowl, combine the
apple, celery, sultanas, peanuts, mayonnaise and salt
and freshly ground black pepper. Stir well to mix.

Pile the apple mixture onto the base of each bagel
and place on individual serving plates. Arrange the
bagel quarters around the bases and serve each one
garnished with a sprig of flat leaf parsley.

THE LONE RANGER

★ ★ ★ ★ ★

A good bonfire-night bagel or a perfect one for the children's supper.

SERVES 4

4 sausages

2 onion bagels

butter or margarine, for spreading

400 g/14 oz can baked beans in tomato sauce

100 g/4 oz Cheddar cheese, grated

METHOD

Grill the sausages for about 10 minutes, turning frequently, until cooked through.

Cut the bagels in half horizontally and toast. Lightly butter the cut surfaces, then place on individual serving plates.

Heat the baked beans in a saucepan. When the sausages are cooked, spoon the baked beans onto the bagel halves and place a sausage on top. Sprinkle over the grated cheese and serve.

GRAND SLAM BAGEL

★ ★ ★ ★ ★

Dripping with juicy meaty flavours, the sautéed mushrooms and melted cheese make this a bagel to remember.

SERVES 2

2 poppy seed bagels

2 minute steaks

175 g/6 oz baby button mushrooms, washed

30–60 ml/2–4 tbsp American mustard

30–60 ml/2–4 tbsp tomato ketchup

salt and freshly ground black pepper

100 g/4 oz mature Cheddar cheese, grated

fresh thyme sprigs, to garnish

METHOD

Cut the bagels in half horizontally and toast. Cut each round in half, to make four crescent shapes.

Heat a non-stick frying pan and dry-fry the steaks with the mushrooms for about 5 minutes, or until the mushrooms have browned and the steak is cooked to your liking. Turn the steaks over halfway through cooking.

Arrange the bottom bagel crescents in an "s" shape on individual serving plates and spread with mustard.

Place a steak on top and then scatter over the mushrooms. Top with ketchup, season with salt and freshly ground black pepper, then position the bagel lids on top.

Sprinkle over the grated cheese. Place the bagels under a hot grill for a few minutes, until the cheese has melted. Serve immediately, garnished with sprigs of fresh thyme.

Grand Slam Bagel

EXOTIC BAGELS

★ ★ ★ ★ ★

TEX MEX BAGEL

★ ★ ★ ★ ★

This chilli-hot filling of tuna, sweetcorn and kidney beans is perfectly complemented by the tangy lemon dressing to cool you down.

SERVES 2

200 g/7 oz can tuna chunks in brine, drained

50 g/2 oz canned sweetcorn kernels, drained

50 g/2 oz canned red kidney beans, drained

pinch of chilli powder

1 bagel

butter or margarine, for spreading

fresh chillies, to garnish

For the dressing

30 ml/2 tbsp olive oil

1 clove of garlic, crushed

15 ml/1 tbsp white wine vinegar

5 ml/1 tsp freshly squeezed lemon juice

15 ml/1 tbsp mayonnaise

salt and freshly ground black pepper

METHOD

To make the filling, place the tuna, sweetcorn and kidney beans in a bowl and combine with the chilli powder. Set aside.

To make the dressing, place all the ingredients in a mixing jug or blender and mix until evenly blended.

Cut the bagel in half horizontally and toast. Lightly butter the cut surfaces and place the bagel halves on individual serving plates.

Spoon the tuna filling on top of each bagel half, then drizzle over the dressing. Serve immediately, garnished with fresh chillies.

PESTO PIZZA BAGEL

★ ★ ★ ★ ★

*A mouth-watering taste of the Mediterranean with plenty of basil
and oregano, this pizza is laced with melted Mozzarella cheese.*

SERVES 2

1 sesame seed bagel

60–75 ml/4–5 tbsp extra virgin olive oil

2 cloves of garlic, quartered

10–15 ml/2–3 tsp tomato purée

25 g/1 oz stoned black olives

2 plum tomatoes, chopped

15 ml/1 tbsp pesto sauce

50 g/2 oz Mozzarella cheese, grated

pinch of dried oregano

salt and freshly ground black pepper

fresh herbs, to garnish

METHOD

Cut the bagel in half horizontally and toast. In a small jug, combine the olive oil and garlic. Stir and leave to stand for about 15 minutes.

Drizzle a little garlic oil over the bagel halves and set aside on a baking sheet.

In a bowl, combine the tomato purée, olives and tomatoes with the pesto sauce. Stir well, then pile onto the bagel halves.

Scatter over the grated Mozzarella cheese, drizzle with remaining garlic oil, discarding the cloves. Sprinkle with oregano and season with salt and freshly ground black pepper.

Bake the pizza bagels in a preheated oven at 200°C/400°F/Gas Mark 6 for about 5–10 minutes, or until the cheese has melted and the bagel bases are crisp. Serve immediately, garnished with fresh herbs.

MILLION DOLLAR BAGEL

★ ★ ★ ★ ★

An elite bagel for a very special occasion.

SERVES 2

1 bagel
butter or margarine, for spreading
2–3 tbsp black caviar
5 ml/1 tsp sour cream
1 hard-boiled egg, shelled and sliced
fresh dill sprigs, to garnish

METHOD

Cut the bagel in half horizontally and lightly butter the cut surfaces.

Spread each bagel half generously with the caviar and level the surface. Use a teaspoon to drizzle over the sour cream in a spiral pattern.

Serve with hard-boiled egg slices, garnished with sprigs of dill.

FESTIVE FILLER

★ ★ ★ ★ ★

Full of the festive spirit, this bagel combines blue cheese, walnuts and grapes. Serve with a glass of port for the perfect snack over the festive season.

SERVES 2

1 bagel
butter or margarine, for spreading
100 g/4 oz blue Stilton cheese, crumbled
50 g/2 oz shelled walnuts, chopped
50 g/2 oz seedless green grapes, peeled and chopped
15–30 ml/1–2 tbsp blue cheese dressing
2 tbsp chopped fresh parsley
salt and freshly ground black pepper

METHOD

Cut the bagel in half horizontally and butter the cut surfaces.

Combine the Stilton, walnuts and grapes in a bowl. Stir in the blue cheese dressing.

Pile the cheese mixture onto the bagel halves and sprinkle over the chopped parsley. Season with salt and freshly ground black pepper and serve.

Million Dollar Bagel

BOMBAY BAGEL

★ ★ ★ ★ ★

*The delicious combination of tomato and egg, draped in a mild and
creamy curried sauce, is dusted with a sprinkling of fresh coriander.*

SERVES 2

1 bagel

butter or margarine, for spreading

2 hard-boiled eggs, shelled and cut into small pieces

75 g/3 oz cherry tomatoes, quartered

15 ml/1 tbsp mild curry paste

45–60 ml/3–4 tbsp mayonnaise

15 ml/1 tbsp milk

2 tbsp chopped fresh coriander

fresh coriander sprigs, to garnish

METHOD

Cut the bagel in half horizontally and lightly butter the
cut surfaces. Cut each half into two equal shapes.

Arrange the pieces of egg and tomato on the bagel
quarters. Mix the curry paste and mayonnaise
together in a small bowl, then stir in the milk.

Drizzle the sauce evenly over the bagels and serve
immediately, sprinkled with chopped fresh coriander
and garnished with a few coriander sprigs.

EL BAGEL

★ ★ ★ ★ ★

A simple yet extremely effective storecupboard party piece, which can be prepared in minutes. Guests will most certainly be impressed.

SERVES 3–4

1 bagel

175 g/6 oz jar pimiento in tomato sauce

olive oil, to drizzle

flat leaf parsley sprig

METHOD

Cut the bagel in half horizontally and toast. Cut each half into quarter pieces.

Top each bagel piece with a teaspoon of pimiento sauce and arrange on a serving plate.

Drizzle with a little olive oil and serve garnished with a sprig of flat leaf parsley.

BANGKOK BAGEL

★ ★ ★ ★ ★

*A Thai salad of tender pieces of chicken, wafer thin slices of carrot
and shredded lettuce, coated in a warm peanut sauce.*

SERVES 2

2 sesame seed bagels

1 cooked chicken breast fillet, skinned and sliced into thin strips

1 small carrot, peeled

½ crisp lettuce heart, shredded

45–60 ml/3–4 tbsp peanut sauce (satay sauce) from a jar

freshly ground black pepper

lemon grass, fresh chillies and coriander, to garnish

METHOD

Cut the bagels in half horizontally and set aside.
  Place the chicken strips in a bowl. Using a vegetable peeler, slice wafer thin strips from the carrot and add to the bowl with the shredded lettuce.
  Warm the peanut sauce in a small saucepan, then add to the bowl. Stir gently to coat the ingredients.
  Pile the salad onto the bagel halves, then season with freshly ground black pepper. Serve garnished with lemon grass, fresh chillies and coriander.

GREENPEACE

★ ★ ★ ★ ★

*The creamy, smooth texture of ripe avocado makes this pale green
topping a delicious dinner party dish.*

SERVES 4

2 bagels

butter or margarine, for spreading

1 ripe avocado, peeled and stoned

freshly squeezed juice of ½ lemon

45–60 ml/3–4 tbsp sour cream

1 tbsp snipped fresh chives

salt and freshly ground black pepper

fresh chives, to garnish

METHOD

Cut the bagels in half horizontally, then cut each half into a crescent. Butter the cut surfaces and set aside.
  Place the avocado in a mixing bowl with the lemon juice, sour cream, snipped chives and salt and freshly ground black pepper. Mash the mixture with a fork or potato masher, until smooth.
  Pile the avocado mixture onto the bagel pieces and arrange on a serving plate. Serve garnished with fresh chives.

Bangkok Bagel

BARBECUE BAGEL

★ ★ ★ ★ ★

Make up your own kebabs using your favourite ingredients. Fish kebabs, using chunks of fish fillet, are extremely tasty.

SERVES 2

4 button mushrooms

¼ red pepper, seeded and cut into pieces

¼ yellow pepper, seeded and cut into pieces

1 large chicken breast fillet, skinned and cut into thin strips

4 cherry tomatoes

1 bagel

butter or margarine, for spreading

few lettuce leaves, to serve

For the marinade

60 ml/4 tbsp olive oil

15 ml/1 tbsp white wine vinegar

5 ml/1 tsp wholegrain mustard

5 ml/1 tsp freshly squeezed lemon juice

salt and freshly ground black pepper

METHOD

To make the kebabs, thread the mushrooms, pepper pieces, chicken and tomatoes onto four small wooden skewers. Lay the kebabs on a baking sheet.

To make the marinade, combine all the ingredients in a small jug and whisk until evenly blended. Pour the marinade over the kebabs and leave for about 15 minutes at room temperature.

Cover the ends of the wooden skewers with small pieces of foil to prevent burning. Grill the kebabs for about 10 minutes, turning frequently in the marinade during cooking, until the chicken is cooked through.

Just before the end of the cooking time, cut the bagel in half horizontally and grill the cut surfaces. Lightly butter and arrange a little lettuce on top. Serve each bagel half with two kebabs, drizzling over any remaining marinade.

FALAFEBAGEL

★ ★ ★ ★ ★

*Falafel are a Middle Eastern speciality made from ground chick
peas and spices. Good packet mixes are available from most supermarkets
and delicatessens, just follow the manufacturers' instructions.*

SERVES 2

16 small falafel balls, made according to the packet
instructions

sunflower oil, for deep frying

1 poppy seed bagel

3–4 tbsp hummus

1 tomato, sliced

7.5 cm/3 in piece of cucumber, finely diced

45–60 ml/3–4 tbsp tahini sauce

1 tbsp chopped fresh mint

fresh mint sprigs, to garnish

METHOD

Deep-fry the falafel balls until crisp and golden. Drain
on absorbent kitchen paper.

Cut the bagel in half horizontally and put each half
on an individual serving plate. Spread the hummus
over each half, then top with the tomato slices.

Place the diced cucumber on top and divide the
falafel balls between them. Drizzle each bagel half
with tahini sauce and sprinkle over the chopped mint.
Garnish with sprigs of fresh mint.

BIARRITZ BAGEL

★ ★ ★ ★ ★

*Where fresh sardines are plump and plentiful – this bagel uses the
convenience variety with all the delicious flavours to remind you of
sunny climes.*

SERVES 2

1 sesame seed bagel

10 ml/2 tsp tomato purée

75 g/3 oz can sardines in oil, drained

1 small tomato, chopped

salt and freshly ground black pepper

pinch of chopped fresh parsley

lemon wedges and flat leaf parsley sprigs, to garnish

METHOD

Cut the bagel in half horizontally and toast the cut
surfaces. Spread the tomato purée over each bagel
half.

Turn the sardines into a bowl and roughly mash with
a fork. Stir in the chopped tomato and season with
salt and freshly ground black pepper.

Pile the sardine mixture onto each bagel half, then
place under a hot grill for about 5 minutes. Serve
sprinkled with chopped parsley and garnished with
lemon wedges and parsley sprigs.

BEIJING BAGEL

★ ★ ★ ★ ★

*With a taste of the Orient, this bagel is topped with a delicately
flavoured combination of stir-fried chicken and vegetables.*

SERVES 2

15 ml/1 tbsp sesame oil

1 clove of garlic, crushed

1 tsp finely grated fresh root ginger

½ orange pepper, seeded and thinly sliced

1 cooked chicken breast fillet, skinned and cut into thin strips

75 g/3 oz baby sweetcorn, cut in half lengthways

3–4 spring onions, cut into thin strips

1 small carrot, finely shredded

50 g/2 oz fresh beansprouts

60–75 ml/4–5 tbsp sweet soy sauce

2 bagels

1 tsp sesame seeds

spring onion tassels and flat leaf parsley sprigs, to garnish

METHOD

To make the stir-fry, heat the sesame oil in a wok or
frying pan and stir-fry the garlic and ginger for about
1 minute.

Add the strips of pepper, then the chicken and
sweetcorn. Stir-fry for about 2–3 minutes, then add
the spring onions, carrot and finally the beansprouts.
Stir and cook for about 1 minute, then sprinkle over
the soy sauce and toss into the ingredients.

Cut the bagels in half horizontally and toast the cut
surfaces. Arrange two halves on each serving plate.

Pile the stir-fry onto the bagels, then sprinkle with
sesame seeds. Garnish with spring onion tassels and
sprigs of flat leaf parsley.

BEVERLY HILLS BAGEL

★ ★ ★ ★

Melba toast bagels are wonderful served with this creamy smoked salmon pâté.

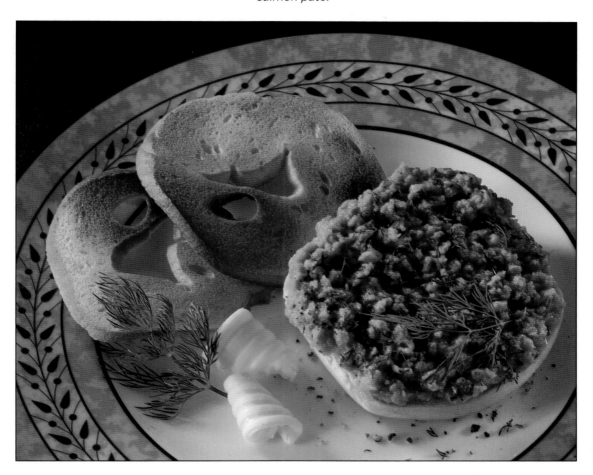

SERVES 2

150 g/5 oz smoked salmon trimmings

30–45 ml/2–3 tbsp double cream

2 tsp chopped fresh dill

few drops of freshly squeezed lemon juice

salt and freshly ground black pepper

2 bagels

butter curls and fresh dill sprigs, to garnish

METHOD

To make the pâté, place the smoked salmon, double cream, chopped dill, lemon juice and salt and ground black pepper in a blender or food processor. Purée until smooth.

Cut the bagels in half horizontally. Slice the top half of each bagel into very thin slices, then toast everything, including the bottoms, on both sides.

Divide the pâté between the bagel bases and serve on individual plates with the "Melba toast" tops, butter curls and sprigs of fresh dill.

Viennese Bagel

RED ALERT

★ ★ ★ ★ ★

Hot and spicy, this red topping is delicious served on a toasted sesame seed bagel.

SERVES 2

15 ml/1 tbsp olive oil

½ red onion, chopped

1 clove of garlic, crushed

½ red pepper, seeded and diced

15 ml/1 tbsp tomato purée

200 g/7 oz can chopped tomatoes, drained

pinch of cayenne pepper

1 tsp cumin seeds

1 tsp mustard seeds

salt and freshly ground black pepper

1 bagel

butter or margarine, for spreading

2–3 tbsp chopped fresh parsley

METHOD

Heat the oil in a frying pan and add the onion, garlic and red pepper. Cook for about 5 minutes, until softened.

Stir in the tomato purée, tomatoes and spices and season with salt and freshly ground black pepper. Cook gently for about 10 minutes, stirring frequently. Allow the mixture to cool.

Meanwhile, cut the bagel in half horizontally and toast. Butter, then top with the red mixture. Serve sprinkled with chopped fresh parsley.

VIENNESE BAGEL

★ ★ ★ ★ ★

A Vienna bagel hot-dog with all the trimmings.

SERVES 2

2 Vienna sausages

15 ml/1 tbsp sunflower oil

1 onion, sliced into thin rings

1 bagel

butter or margarine, for spreading

30–45 ml/2–3 tbsp American mustard

30–45 ml/2–3 tbsp tomato ketchup

salt and freshly ground black pepper

pickles, to serve

METHOD

Place the Viennas in boiling water for about 5 minutes, or until heated through. Drain.

Meanwhile, heat the oil in a frying pan and fry the onion rings for about 5 minutes, until slightly golden.

Cut the bagel in half vertically then slice each crescent horizontally, almost right through. Lightly butter the cut surfaces.

To assemble the bagel halves place them, cut side up, on an individual serving plate. Place a Vienna in the middle of each bagel half to resemble a hot-dog roll.

Scatter a few fried onions on top of the Viennas, then add the mustard and ketchup. Season with salt and freshly ground black pepper. Serve with pickles.

Viennese Bagel

FILET DE BAGEL

★ ★ ★ ★ ★

A fillet steak bagel fit for a dinner party. Serve with tender sweet carrots and sautéed potatoes.

SERVES 4

50 g/2 oz butter or margarine

225 g/8 oz button mushrooms, sliced

4 small fillet steaks

1–2 tsp dried thyme

salt and freshly ground black pepper

2 sesame seed bagels

60 ml/4 tbsp Béarnaise sauce

fresh thyme sprigs, to garnish

METHOD

Melt the butter or margarine in a large frying pan and sauté the mushrooms for about 5 minutes.

Move the mushrooms to the side of the pan and add the steaks. Sprinkle over the thyme and season with salt and freshly ground black pepper. Cook for 5–10 minutes, depending on how rare you like your meat, turning the steaks over halfway through cooking.

Meanwhile, cut the bagels in half horizontally and toast the cut surfaces. Using a pastry brush, spread some of the cooking juices from the frying pan over the cut surfaces of the bagels.

Warm the Bearnaise sauce in a small saucepan. To serve the bagels, place the halves on individual serving plates, top with mushrooms, then a piece of steak.

Drizzle over the Béarnaise sauce and season with a little extra ground black pepper. Garnish with sprigs of fresh thyme.

POSH NOSH BAGEL

★ ★ ★ ★ ★

*This warm goats' cheese salad with a special dressing is served on
a lightly toasted bagel. It makes an excellent starter for a dinner party.*

SERVES 4

2 bagels

butter or margarine, for spreading

4 × 2.5 cm/1 in slices of goats' cheese

few mixed salad leaves

flat leaf parsley sprigs, to garnish

For the dressing

30 ml/2 tbsp hazelnut oil

60 ml/4 tbsp sunflower oil

30–45 ml/2–3 tbsp white wine vinegar

5 ml/1 tsp English mustard

salt and freshly ground black pepper

METHOD

To make the dressing, combine all the ingredients in a mixing jug and whisk until evenly blended. Set aside.

Cut the bagels in half horizontally and lightly toast the cut surfaces, then butter them.

Arrange the goats' cheese slices on a sheet of foil on a baking sheet. Place under a hot grill for about 2–3 minutes, or until just melting and golden.

Place one cheese on each bagel half and place on individual serving plates with a few salad leaves. Pour over the dressing and serve immediately, garnished with sprigs of flat leaf parsley.

GUACABAGEL

★ ★ ★ ★ ★

An inventive way of serving bagels – the channelling out enables the flavours of the guacamole filling to seep into the walls of the bagel and taste really scrumptious.

SERVES 2

1 avocado, peeled and stoned

½ small onion, finely chopped

1 small clove of garlic, crushed

1 tomato, chopped

squeeze of fresh lemon juice

salt and freshly ground black pepper

pinch of chilli powder

2 poppy seed bagels

paprika, for dusting

flat leaf parsley and chillies, to garnish

METHOD

To make the guacamole, put the avocado, onion, garlic, tomato, lemon juice, salt and freshly ground black pepper and chilli powder in a blender or food processor. Purée until smooth.

Using a small, sharp knife, cut about 0.5–1cm/ ¼–½in down into the top of each bagel, very close to the outside edge. Cut all around the bagel. Repeat the process around the inside edge.

Cut out the inside section, to make a hollowed out channel, running round the bagel. Fill the bagel channels with the guacamole. Serve sprinkled with paprika. Garnish with sprigs of flat leaf parsley and chillies.

PALM BEACH BAGEL

★ ★ ★ ★ ★

Light and refreshing, this exotic salad of chicken, pineapple and
coconut is complemented by the cool taste of fresh mint.

SERVES 2

2 sesame seed bagels

30 ml/2 tbsp mayonnaise

1 cooked chicken breast fillet, skinned and diced

75 g/3 oz canned pineapple, drained and thinly sliced

25 g/1 oz flaked coconut, toasted

fresh mint sprigs, to garnish

For the dressing

45 ml/3 tbsp hazelnut oil

15 ml/1 tbsp white wine vinegar

salt and freshly ground black pepper

2 tbsp chopped fresh mint

METHOD

Cut around the inside of each bagel, slightly in from the edge. Scoop out the middle section of dough to make a hollow.

Line the inside of the bagels with the mayonnaise, spreading it evenly with the back of a teaspoon.

Combine the chicken, pineapple and coconut in a bowl. Mix together the dressing ingredients and pour over the chicken mixture.

Toss the filling to coat in the dressing, then pile into the bagels. Garnish with sprigs of fresh mint.

AUBERBAGEL

★ ★ ★ ★ ★

*This creamy aubergine topping is perfect served on warm fresh
bagels for lunch or as an appetizer.*

SERVES 2–4

1 bagel

30 ml/2 tbsp olive oil

2 cloves of garlic, crushed

1 small onion, finely chopped

1 small aubergine, cut into small pieces

150 ml/¼ pint double cream

salt and freshly ground black pepper

1–2 tbsp chopped fresh parsley

tomato wedges and fresh parsley sprigs, to garnish

METHOD

Cut the bagel in half horizontally, then cut each half vertically into crescents.

Heat the oil in a frying pan and add the garlic and onion. Sauté for about 5 minutes, until the onion has softened. Add the aubergine pieces and cook for about 5–7 minutes, until the aubergine is cooked and browned.

Stir in the cream and season with salt and freshly ground black pepper. Simmer for about 5 minutes, then cool slightly.

Serve the aubergine mixture spooned onto the bagel crescents. Sprinkle over the chopped parsley and serve with tomato wedges and sprigs of parsley, to garnish.

VEGETARIAN
BAGELS

★ ★ ★ ★ ★

MEDITERRANEAN BAGEL

★ ★ ★ ★ ★

*Full of the flavours of the sun, this pepper, aubergine and tomato
filling is lightly cooked in virgin olive oil and garlic.*

SERVES 2

45 ml/3 tbsp extra virgin olive oil

2 cloves of garlic, crushed

½ red pepper, seeded and chopped

½ yellow pepper, seeded and chopped

½ small aubergine, cut into small pieces

25 g/1 oz sun dried tomatoes, chopped

30 ml/2 tbsp tomato purée

30 ml/2 tbsp dry red wine

salt and freshly ground black pepper

1 poppy seed bagel

2–3 tbsp chopped fresh parsley and basil

25 g/1 oz freshly grated Parmesan cheese

fresh basil leaves, to garnish

METHOD

Heat the oil in a large frying pan and add the garlic,
peppers and aubergine. Cook for about 5 minutes, or
until softened and lightly browned.

Add the sun dried tomatoes, tomato purée, red
wine and season with salt and freshly ground black
pepper. Cook for another 5 minutes, stirring
frequently. Cool slightly.

Meanwhile, cut the bagel in half horizontally and
toast. Top each bagel half with the aubergine mixture
and sprinkle with chopped fresh herbs. Scatter over
the Parmesan cheese and serve garnished with fresh
basil leaves.

TAVERNA BAGEL

★ ★ ★ ★

A traditional combination of Greek salad ingredients, coated in an olive oil and lemon dressing.

SERVES 2

1 bagel

butter or margarine, for spreading

75 g/3 oz feta cheese, cut into small cubes

10 cm/4 in piece of cucumber, cut into small cubes

1 plum tomato, cut into pieces

50 g/2 oz stoned black olives

chopped fresh mint, finely grated lemon zest, fresh mint sprigs and salad leaves, to garnish

For the dressing

1 clove of garlic, crushed

45 ml/3 tbsp extra virgin olive oil

15–30 ml/1–2 tbsp white wine vinegar

5 ml/1 tsp freshly squeezed lemon juice

salt and freshly ground black pepper

METHOD

Cut the bagel in half horizontally and butter the cut surfaces. Combine the feta cheese, cucumber, tomato and olives in a mixing bowl.

To make the dressing, place the garlic, oil, vinegar, lemon juice and salt and freshly ground black pepper in a mixing bowl. Whisk, then pour over the salad ingredients.

Divide the salad mixture between the bagel halves. Serve sprinkled with chopped fresh mint and lemon zest and garnish with a few sprigs of fresh mint and some salad leaves.

SPROUTING BAGEL

★ ★ ★ ★ ★

*One for the health-conscious, this bagel is filled
with low-fat cheese and sprouting seeds.*

SERVES 2

1 onion bagel

4 tbsp low-fat cream cheese

15 g/½ oz alfalfa sprouts

15 g/½ oz beansprouts

25 g/1 oz cherry tomatoes, quartered

30 ml/2 tbsp French dressing

salt and freshly ground black pepper

METHOD

Cut the bagel in half horizontally and toast. Divide the
cream cheese between the bagel halves and spread
evenly.

Place the alfalfa and beansprouts in a bowl with
the cherry tomato quarters. Toss to combine.

Divide the sprout mixture between the bagel
halves. Sprinkle over the French dressing and season
with salt and freshly ground black pepper to taste.

SUNSET BOULEVARD

★ ★ ★ ★ ★

*A deliciously light and tangy combination of
beetroot and orange, with the crunch of pine nuts.*

SERVES 2

1 sesame seed bagel

butter or margarine, for spreading

100 g/4 oz cooked beetroot, peeled and diced

2 small sweet oranges, segmented

1 tbsp pine nuts

finely grated orange zest, fresh mint leaves and sprigs, to
garnish

For the dressing

30 ml/2 tbsp hazelnut oil

15 ml/1 tbsp fresh orange juice

10 ml/2 tsp white wine vinegar

salt and freshly ground black pepper

METHOD

Cut the bagel in half horizontally and butter the cut
surfaces. Place the beetroot, orange segments and
pine nuts in a bowl.

To make the dressing, mix together the hazelnut oil,
orange juice and vinegar. Season with salt and freshly
ground black pepper and pour over the beetroot
mixture. Toss the salad gently.

Pile the beetroot and orange mixture onto the
bagel halves. Scatter over a little orange zest and a
few mint leaves. Serve garnished with extra sprigs of
fresh mint.

Sunset Boulevard

VEGETARIAN FRIDAY NIGHT BAGEL

★ ★ ★ ★ ★

*A vegetarian alternative to chopped liver. This unusual chestnut
recipe is so delicious, it might even convert a few carnivores.*

SERVES 4

15 ml/1 tbsp olive oil

1 small onion, finely chopped

1 clove of garlic, crushed

450 g/1 lb can chestnuts

60–75 ml/4–5 tbsp dry red wine

salt and freshly ground black pepper

2 sesame seed bagels

butter or margarine, for spreading

1 hard-boiled egg

2 tbsp chopped fresh parsley

fresh parsley sprigs, to garnish

METHOD

Heat the oil in a frying pan and add the onion and
garlic. Cook for about 5 minutes, until the onion has
softened. Add the chestnuts and wine, stir well and
cook gently for about 10 minutes, stirring
occasionally.

Transfer the chestnut mixture to a food processor
or blender and purée until you have the desired
texture. Season with salt and freshly ground black
pepper, then cool.

Cut the bagels in half horizontally and butter the cut
surfaces. Divide the pâté between the bagel halves,
smoothing it out evenly.

Separate the egg white from the yolk and press
separately through a sieve or tea-strainer. Use the
sieved egg white and yolk to make alternate lines
across the pâté. Sprinkle with chopped parsley and
serve each half garnished with a parsley sprig.

VIVA ESPAÑA

★ ★ ★ ★ ★

A small omelette is perfect for this recipe for one. Alternatively make a larger omelette and serve cut into wedges.

SERVES 1

25 g/1 oz butter

¼ small onion, finely chopped

1 small potato, peeled and diced

⅛ red pepper, seeded and diced

⅛ yellow pepper, seeded and diced

1 tbsp chopped fresh parsley

salt and freshly ground black pepper

2 eggs, beaten

1 poppy seed bagel

butter or margarine, for spreading

2 tsp finely grated Cheddar cheese

pickled chillies and fresh flat leaf parsley sprig, to garnish

METHOD

Melt the butter in a small frying pan and add the onion, potato, peppers and all but a pinch of the parsley. Cook gently for about 10 minutes, stirring frequently, until the potato is cooked and browned.

Season the vegetables with salt and freshly ground black pepper, then pour in the beaten eggs. Cook the omelette on one side and grill the other, until golden.

Meanwhile, cut the bagel in half horizontally and toast. Butter the cut surfaces and sandwich the omelette in between the two halves.

Sprinkle the lid of the bagel with the reserved pinch of chopped parsley and the grated cheese. Garnish with pickled chillies and a sprig of flat leaf parsley.

TZATZIKI BAGEL

★ ★ ★ ★ ★

*Perfect for a hot summer's day, the tzatziki mixture can be made in
advance and kept in the fridge. Use to fill the bagels
just before serving.*

SERVES 2

225 g/8 oz Greek yoghurt

10 cm/4 in piece of cucumber, peeled and finely diced

3–4 cloves of garlic, crushed

3 tbsp chopped fresh mint

salt and freshly ground black pepper

1 onion bagel

fresh mint sprigs, to garnish

METHOD

Put the yoghurt in a mixing bowl and stir in the cucumber, garlic and mint. Season with salt and freshly ground black pepper. Cover and chill for at least 1 hour.

Cut the bagel in half horizontally and toast. Divide the tzatziki between the bagel halves. Serve garnished with sprigs of fresh mint.

WILD WEST BAGEL

★ ★ ★ ★ ★

*Any combination of mushrooms is suitable for this recipe. Just
remember to cook the more delicate mushrooms last.*

SERVES 2

50 g/2 oz butter or margarine

2 cloves of garlic, crushed

2 tsp dried thyme

175 g/6 oz mixed mushrooms, including shiitake, oyster and chestnut, washed and sliced if appropriate

1 bagel

salt and freshly ground black pepper

fresh thyme sprigs, to garnish

METHOD

Melt the butter in a frying pan and add the garlic and thyme. Cook for about 1 minute, then add the mushrooms. Sauté the mushrooms, stirring frequently, for about 5 minutes, until slightly browned.

Meanwhile, cut the bagel in half horizontally and toast. Divide the mushroom mixture between the bagel halves and season with salt and freshly ground black pepper.

Garnish with sprigs of fresh thyme.

Wild West Bagel

VEGGIE BURGER BAGEL

★ ★ ★ ★ ★

Liven up your favourite veggie burger and serve it on a toasted sesame bagel, with all the trimmings, of course!

SERVES 2

2 veggie burgers

2 sesame seed bagels

butter or margarine, for spreading

30 ml/2 tbsp mayonnaise

1 tomato, sliced

30–45 ml/2–3 tbsp tomato ketchup

a few lettuce leaves

salad leaves and fresh herbs, to garnish

METHOD

Cook the veggie burgers according to the manufacturer's instructions.

Meanwhile, cut the bagels in half horizontally and lightly toast. Butter the cut surfaces and place the bagel bases on individual serving plates.

To assemble the burger bagels, place a dollop of mayonnaise on each base and spread out evenly. Top with a few slices of tomato, then a little ketchup, followed by the veggie burger.

Add a few lettuce leaves, a little more ketchup, if you like, then place the bagel top in position. Serve with a few extra salad leaves and fresh herbs, to garnish.

VEGETARIAN DREAM

★ ★ ★ ★

Bean pâté is available from most supermarkets and health food shops, but you can use your own favourite variety of spread or pâté.

SERVES 2

2 poppy seed bagels

butter or margarine, for spreading

100 g/4 oz bean pâté

½ large avocado, peeled and sliced

30–45 ml/2–3 tbsp mayonnaise

200 g/7 oz can mixed beans in water, drained

30 ml/2 tbsp French dressing

10 ml/2 tsp tomato purée

salt and freshly ground black pepper

flat leaf parsley sprigs, to garnish

METHOD

Cut the bagels horizontally into three layers and butter.

Divide the bean pâté between the bottom layers, then top with the sliced avocado. Spoon some mayonnaise on top, then position the middle layers.

Put the mixed beans in a bowl. Whisk the French dressing together with the tomato purée, then pour over the beans.

Divide the bean mixture between the bagels, then season with salt and freshly ground black pepper. Position the bagel lids and serve garnished with sprigs of flat parsley.

71

SUPER SUPPER BAGEL

★ ★ ★ ★ ★

This lentil and nut filled bagel is a meal in itself. Serve with a crisp salad and a glass of chilled white wine for the perfect meal.

SERVES 2

1 large bagel

30 ml/2 tbsp olive oil

1 clove of garlic, crushed

2 tsp dried thyme

100 g/4 oz mushrooms, chopped

75 g/3 oz cooked green lentils, drained

25 g/1 oz chopped cashew nuts, toasted

25 g/1 oz plain wholewheat flour

200 ml/7fl oz milk

100 g/4 oz mature Cheddar cheese, grated

salt and freshly ground black pepper

fresh thyme sprigs, to garnish

METHOD

Cut the bagel in half horizontally and remove the inner dough to make a hollow. Place the hollowed bagel halves in a shallow ovenproof dish.

Heat the oil in a frying pan and add the garlic and thyme. Cook for about 1 minute, then add the mushrooms. Cook for about 5 minutes, then stir in the lentils and cashew nuts. Continue to cook for 2–3 minutes.

Sprinkle over the flour and stir in well. Gradually pour in the milk, stirring continuously, until blended. Bring to the boil, stirring. Stir in the cheese until melted and season with salt and freshly ground black pepper.

Spoon the mixture into the hollowed bagels and around the edges in the dish. Bake in a preheated oven at 190°C/375°F/Gas Mark 5 for about 15–20 minutes, until the filling is golden. Serve immediately, garnished with sprigs of fresh thyme.

EASTERN PROMISE

★ ★ ★ ★ ★

Based on the traditional Middle Eastern speciality, Tabbouleh, the bulgar wheat needs to soak for at least 20 minutes in boiling water.

SERVES 4

75 g/3 oz bulgar wheat, soaked and drained

few spring onions, chopped

2 tomatoes, sliced into wedges

25 g/1 oz black olives, stoned and quartered

5 tbsp chopped fresh mint

60 ml/4 tbsp extra virgin olive oil

15 ml/1 tbsp freshly squeezed lemon juice

2 cloves of garlic, finely chopped

salt and freshly ground black pepper

2 bagels

butter or margarine, for spreading

finely grated zest of 1 lemon

fresh mint sprigs and tomato slices, to garnish

METHOD

Place the bulgar wheat in a bowl with the spring onions, tomatoes, olives and mint. Drizzle over the olive oil and lemon juice, then stir in the chopped garlic. Season with salt and freshly ground black pepper. Mix well.

Cut the bagels in half horizontally and toast. Butter the cut surfaces and place on individual serving plates.

Top each bagel half generously with the bulgar mixture, then sprinkle over a little lemon zest. Serve garnished with sprigs of fresh mint and tomato slices.

Eastern Promise

THE BIG CHEESE

★ ★ ★ ★ ★

*Crisp on the outside with soft, warm, melted cheese on the inside,
this lightly toasted bagel is served with the sharp, sweet contrast of
gooseberry sauce.*

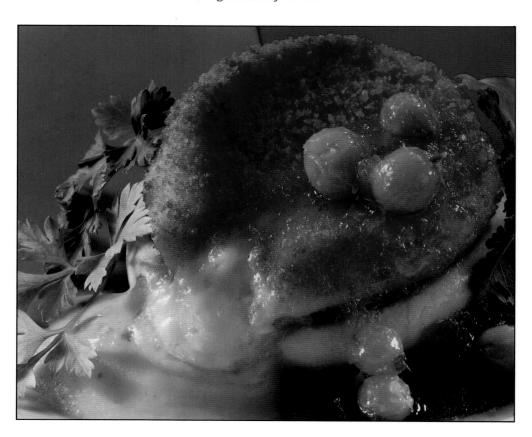

SERVES 2

2 whole individual Camembert cheeses

1 egg, beaten

75 g/3 oz fine breadcrumbs

1 bagel

butter or margarine, for spreading

30 ml/2 tbsp gooseberry jam

50 g/2 oz gooseberries in syrup, from a jar

fresh flat parsley sprigs, to garnish

METHOD

Coat the Camembert cheeses in the beaten egg, then
in the breadcrumbs. Place on a baking sheet and bake
in a preheated oven at 180°C/350°F/Gas Mark 4 for
about 10–15 minutes, or until the cheese is warmed
and melting.

Meanwhile, cut the bagel in half horizontally and
toast. Butter the cut surfaces.

Warm the gooseberry jam in a small saucepan and
add the gooseberries with about 45 ml/3 tbsp syrup.

Serve a Camembert cheese on each bagel half,
with the gooseberry sauce as an accompaniment.
Garnish with sprigs of fresh flat parsley.

BAGEL SKINS

★ ★ ★ ★ ★

*Crispy and crunchy, naughty but nice – choose your favourite filling
to suit your taste.*

SERVES 2

2 bagels

vegetable oil, for deep frying

225 g/8 oz guacamole

100 g/4 oz Cheddar cheese, grated

pinch of paprika

fresh parsley sprigs, to garnish

METHOD

Cut the bagels in half vertically and pull out the dough from the middle, making a hollow crescent.

Heat the oil to 170°C/325°F for deep frying. Fry the bagel crescents for about 5 minutes, until crisp and golden. Drain on absorbent kitchen paper.

Fill each crescent with guacamole, then top with grated cheese and paprika. Place on a baking sheet and grill for about 1 minute to melt the cheese. Serve immediately, garnished with sprigs of fresh parsley.

MEATLESS MAGIC

★ ★ ★ ★ ★

This is a tempting vegetarian bagel which even meat eaters will love.

SERVES 2

sunflower oil, for shallow frying

100 g/4 oz marinated tofu, cut into thin strips

1 clove of garlic, crushed

15 ml/1 tbsp curry paste

75 g/3 oz baby sweetcorn

50 g/2 oz mangetouts

¼ red pepper, seeded and cut into thin strips

150 ml/¼ pint vegetable stock

4 tbsp dessicated coconut

3 tbsp chopped fresh coriander

1 bagel

fresh coriander sprigs, to garnish

METHOD

Heat the oil for shallow frying and fry the tofu strips for about 3–5 minutes, turning them over, until crisp and golden. Drain on absorbent kitchen paper.

Carefully transfer about 30 ml/2 tbsp of the cooking oil to another frying pan and cook the garlic for about 1 minute. Stir in the curry paste and cook for a further minute.

Add the vegetables and cook for about 5 minutes, stirring frequently. Add the stock and coconut powder and cook gently for about 5 minutes, until the vegetables are just tender and the sauce has thickened.

Stir in the tofu strips and fresh coriander for the last minute of the cooking time.

Meanwhile, cut the bagel in half horizontally and lightly toast. Place the bagel halves on individual serving plates and top with the creamy tofu and vegetable mixture. Serve immediately, garnished with sprigs of fresh coriander.

ROCK 'N' ROLL BAGEL

★ ★ ★ ★ ★

A rich combination of leeks, mushrooms and tomatoes with Roquefort cheese.

SERVES 2

30 ml/2 tbsp olive oil

1 clove of garlic, crushed

1 tbsp chopped fresh rosemary

½ leek, thinly sliced

50 g/2 oz mushrooms, quartered

50 g/2 oz cherry tomatoes, quartered

50 g/2 oz Roquefort cheese, crumbled

2 bagels

butter or margarine, for spreading

fresh rosemary sprigs, to garnish

METHOD

Heat the oil in a frying pan and add the garlic and chopped rosemary. Cook for about 1 minute.

Add the leek and mushrooms and continue to cook for about 5 minutes, or until the vegetables are lightly browned. Add the cherry tomatoes and Roquefort cheese and cook for a further minute.

Meanwhile, cut the bagels in half horizontally and toast. Butter the cut surfaces. Serve on individual plates with the Roquefort filling. Garnish with sprigs of fresh rosemary.

Rock 'n' Roll Bagel

SUMMER BREEZE

★ ★ ★ ★ ★

Tender cooked vegetable filling, coated in a light dressing and tossed together with sunflower seeds and freshly grated Parmesan cheese, all served on a lightly toasted bagel.

SERVES 2

175 g/6 oz fresh asparagus tips, trimmed

1 carrot, peeled and thinly sliced

30 ml/2 tbsp hazelnut oil

15 ml/1 tbsp sunflower oil·

15 ml/1 tbsp white wine vinegar

10 ml/2 tsp fresh orange juice

salt and freshly ground black pepper

2 tbsp toasted sunflower seeds

1 sesame seed bagel

butter or margarine, for spreading

25 g/1 oz freshly grated Parmesan cheese

fresh herb sprigs, to garnish

METHOD

Place the asparagus and sliced carrot in a steamer or small amount of water and cook for about 5 minutes, until just tender. Drain, if necessary. Place the vegetables in a bowl.

Mix together the hazelnut and sunflower oils, vinegar and orange juice. Pour over the vegetables and toss to coat. Season with salt and freshly ground black pepper, then stir in the sunflower seeds.

Cut the bagel in half horizontally and lightly toast. Butter the cut surfaces and place on individual serving plates.

Arrange the vegetable mixture on top of each bagel half, then spoon over any remaining dressing. Sprinkle with Parmesan cheese and serve garnished with sprigs of fresh herbs.

HOMETY BAGEL

★ ★ ★ ★ ★

A warm, filling bagel, perfect served with lightly cooked carrots for a special supper-time treat.

SERVES 2

2 bagels

2 large potatoes, peeled and cut into pieces

100 g/4 oz cauliflower florets

50 g/2 oz butter or margarine

salt and freshly ground black pepper

75 g/3 oz mature Cheddar cheese, grated

2 tsp chopped fresh parsley, to garnish

METHOD

Cut a thin slice horizontally off the top of the bagel. Pull out the dough from the inside of the bagel to make a hollow ring.

Simmer the potatoes and cauliflower separately in boiling water, until the potatoes are cooked and the cauliflower is just tender. Drain.

Mash the potatoes with the butter, salt and freshly ground black pepper and all but 25 g/1 oz of the grated cheese. Carefully stir in the cauliflower florets, without breaking them.

Pile the potato mixture into each bagel, then top with the reserved grated cheese.

Place the bagels on a baking sheet and cook in a preheated oven at 200°C/400°F/Gas Mark 6 for about 15–20 minutes, until the filling is golden and the bagel is crisp. Serve garnished with chopped parsley.

SQUASHED BAGEL

★ ★ ★ ★ ★

Any combination of squashes works well for this recipe. Remember the more colourful, the more attractive the finished result will be.

SERVES 4

450 g/1 lb mixed squashes, such as pumpkin, acorn, prince etc., peeled and diced

50 g/2 oz butter

2 cloves of garlic, crushed

squeeze of fresh lemon juice

3 tbsp chopped fresh dill

4 bagels

butter or margarine, for spreading

50 g/2 oz red Leicester cheese, grated

salt and freshly ground black pepper

fresh dill sprigs, to garnish

METHOD

Cook the diced squashes in boiling water or steam for about 5 minutes, or until just tender. Drain well.

Melt the butter in a frying pan and sauté the garlic for about 1 minute. Add the cooked squashes, with the lemon juice and chopped dill. Cook for about 3–5 minutes.

Meanwhile, cut the bagels in half horizontally and toast. Butter the bases, then place them on individual serving plates.

Arrange the bagel tops on a baking sheet and sprinkle over the grated cheese. Place under a hot grill, until melted.

Divide the squash mixture between the bagel bases and season with salt and freshly ground black pepper. Top each one with a cheese covered lid and garnish with a sprig of fresh dill.

RATABAGEL

★ ★ ★ ★ ★

*This traditional mixture of vegetables, cooked in a rich garlicky
tomato sauce, is perfect served with a toasted bagel to mop up the
delicious juices.*

SERVES 2

45 ml/3 tbsp olive oil

2 cloves of garlic, crushed

½ onion, sliced

½ red pepper, seeded and cut into pieces

½ yellow pepper, seeded and cut into pieces

1 courgette, cut into pieces

1 tomato, cut into wedges

3–4 tbsp chopped fresh parsley

150 ml/¼ pint vegetable stock

45 ml/3 tbsp tomato purée

salt and freshly ground black pepper

1 sesame seed bagel

fresh flat leaf parsley sprigs, to garnish

METHOD

Heat the oil in a large frying pan and add the garlic
and onion. Fry for about 3 minutes, until the onion has
browned. Add the peppers and courgette and
continue to cook for a further 5 minutes.

Add the tomato, chopped parsley, stock and
tomato purée and season with salt and freshly ground
black pepper. Cover and cook gently for about 10–15
minutes, stirring frequently.

Cut the bagel in half horizontally and toast. Cut
each half into two equal portions and serve with the
ratatouille mixture. Garnish with a sprig of fresh flat
leaf parsley.

SWEET BAGELS

★ ★ ★ ★ ★

BREAD 'N' BUTTER BAGEL

★ ★ ★ ★ ★

Serve this warm and filling pudding bagel with custard or whipped cream.

SERVES 2

2 cinnamon and raisin bagels

1 egg, beaten

finely grated zest of ½ lemon

4 tbsp caster sugar

2 tbsp sultanas

pinch of grated nutmeg

15 g/½ oz melted butter

45 ml/3 tbsp milk

METHOD

Cut a thin slice off the top of each bagel and scoop out the dough from the middle with your fingers, making a hollow channel. Place the scooped-out dough in a mixing bowl and put the hollowed out bagels in a shallow ovenproof dish.

Add the beaten egg to the bagel dough in the mixing bowl, with the lemon zest, sugar, sultanas, nutmeg, melted butter and milk. Mix well.

Spoon the egg mixture into the hollowed bagels. Bake in a preheated oven at 190°C/375°F/Gas Mark 5 for about 25–30 minutes, or until the mixture is golden. Serve immediately.

ORANGE LOCKSHEN PUDDING BAGEL

★ ★ ★ ★ ★

Based on the Jewish theme, this bagel uses a little creative licence, resulting in a real bagel speciality.

SERVES 2

2 cinnamon and raisin bagels

25 g/1 oz butter or margarine, melted

1 egg

50 g/2 oz caster sugar

pinch of ground cinnamon

finely grated zest of ½ orange

few drops of orange essence

2 tbsp sultanas

50 g/2 oz vermicelli pasta, broken into small pieces, cooked in boiling water and drained

sifted icing sugar, to decorate

METHOD

Cut a thin slice off the top of each bagel and scoop out the dough from the middle with your fingers, to make a hollow channel. Discard the dough and top. Place the hollowed bagels in a shallow ovenproof dish.

Using a pastry brush, coat the inside of each hollowed bagel with a little of the melted butter.

Place the egg and sugar in a mixing bowl and whisk, using an electric hand mixer, until frothy. Whisk in the cinnamon, orange zest and essence. Add the sultanas and cooked vermicelli to the whisked mixture and stir to coat evenly.

Spoon the vermicelli mixture into the hollowed bagels. Bake in a preheated oven at 190°C/375°F/ Gas Mark 5 for about 25–30 minutes, or until the mixture is set and golden. Serve warm, dusted generously with sifted icing sugar.

BANANA BAGEL SPLIT

★ ★ ★ ★

A rich banana and cream topped bagel – ideal for adults and children alike.

SERVES 2

1 cinnamon and raisin bagel

300ml/½ pint double cream

3 tbsp sifted icing sugar

few drops of banana essence

2 bananas, peeled and cut in half lengthways

30–45 ml/2–3 tbsp maple syrup

coloured hundreds and thousands, to decorate

METHOD

Cut the bagel in half horizontally and toast. Keep warm.

Put the cream in a bowl with the icing sugar and banana essence. Whisk, using an electric hand mixer, until it holds soft peaks.

Place the bagel halves on individual serving plates and divide about two-thirds of the cream mixture between them.

Lay the split bananas on top of the cream, then top with the remaining cream mixture. Drizzle with maple syrup, then sprinkle with hundreds and thousands, to decorate.

PEANUT CHOCCA BAGEL

★ ★ ★ ★ ★

A perfect tea-time treat for kids.

SERVES 2

2 cinnamon and raisin bagels

butter or margarine, for spreading

60–75 ml/4–5 tbsp crunchy peanut butter spread

45–60 ml/3–4 tbsp chocolate spread

2 tbsp sifted chocolate powder, to decorate

METHOD

Cut each bagel horizontally to make three even layers and butter.

Divide the peanut butter between the two bagel bases and spread evenly. Place the middle bagel layer on top of the peanut butter and smooth over the chocolate spread.

Top with the bagel lid and serve dusted with sifted chocolate powder.

CHOCOLATE DREAM

★ ★ ★ ★ ★

This bagel, for chocaholics, deserves the very best quality chocolate ice-cream topping. It is even covered in chocolate sauce.

SERVES 2

1 cinnamon and raisin bagel

4 scoops of chocolate ice-cream

60–75 ml/4–5 tbsp chocolate sauce

2–3 tbsp grated dessert chocolate, to decorate

METHOD

Cut the bagel in half horizontally and toast. Place each half on an individual serving plate.

Place two scoops of chocolate ice-cream on each bagel half, while the bagel is still warm.

Drizzle over the chocolate sauce and serve immediately, sprinkled with grated chocolate.

Chocolate Dream

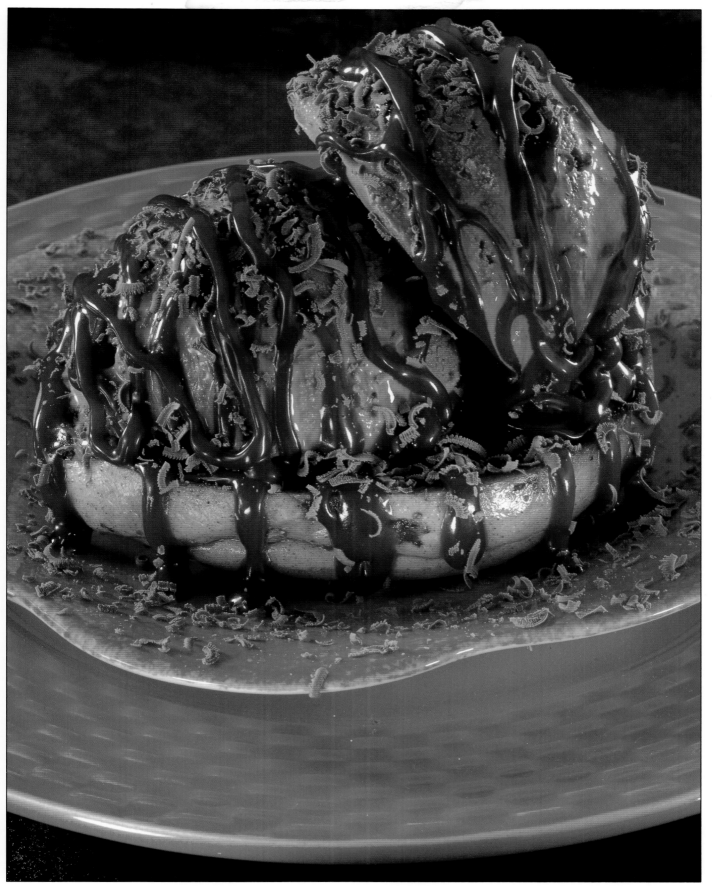

BAGELOVA

★ ★ ★ ★ ★

*Based on the traditional Pavlova idea, this bagel is quick and simple
to prepare and tastes delicious.*

SERVES 2

1 cinnamon and raisin bagel

150 ml/¼ pint double cream

2 tbsp sifted icing sugar, plus extra for dusting

few drops of vanilla essence

225 g/8 oz mixed soft fruits, such as blueberries, raspberries,
chopped strawberries and kiwi

fresh mint sprigs, to decorate

METHOD

Cut the bagel in half horizontally and place on individual serving plates.

Put the cream in a mixing bowl and add the icing sugar and vanilla essence. Whisk with an electric hand mixer until it holds soft peaks.

Divide the cream mixture between the bagel halves, then pile the mixed fruit on top. Dust generously with sifted icing sugar and serve immediately, decorated with sprigs of fresh mint.

BAGEL HÉLÈNE

★ ★ ★ ★ ★

*A traditional dessert duo of pears and chocolate sauce, served on
a sweet soft bagel, topped with whipped cream.*

SERVES 2

1 cinnamon and raisin bagel

150 ml/¼ pint double cream

1 tbsp sifted icing sugar

few drops of vanilla essence

4 canned pear halves in syrup, drained

60–75 ml/4–5 tbsp chocolate sauce

tiny lemon geranium or fresh mint sprigs, to decorate

METHOD

Cut the bagel in half horizontally and place on individual serving plates.

Put the cream in a mixing bowl and add the icing sugar and vanilla essence. Whisk, using an electric hand mixer, until it forms soft peaks.

Divide the cream mixture between the bagel bases and spread out evenly. Top with the pear halves, then drizzle generously with chocolate sauce. Decorate with tiny sprigs of lemon geranium or mint. Serve immediately.

SUNSHINE BAGEL

★ ★ ★ ★ ★

An elegant and original dinner party dessert to stun your guests.

SERVES 4

2 cinnamon and raisin bagels

425 ml/¾ pint double cream

4 tbsp icing sugar, sifted

few drops of vanilla essence

15 ml/1 tbsp Cointreau liqueur

4 small caramelized oranges in syrup, drained (reserving 200 ml/7 fl oz syrup) and sliced

1½ tbsp arrowroot

finely grated orange zest and fresh mint sprigs, to decorate

METHOD

Cut the bagels in half horizontally and place on individual serving plates.

Put the cream in a mixing bowl and add the icing sugar, vanilla essence and Cointreau. Whisk with an electric hand mixer until it holds soft peaks.

Use the cream mixture to fill a piping bag fitted with a medium star nozzle. Pipe decoratively on top of each bagel half.

Arrange the sliced oranges on top of the cream, then finish piping decoratively on top.

Mix enough of the reserved orange syrup with the arrowroot to make a smooth paste. Heat the remaining syrup in a small saucepan, until boiling. Stir in the arrowroot paste and return to the boil, stirring continuously, until thickened, shiny and smooth. Cool slightly.

Drizzle the orange sauce over the bagel halves. Decorate with orange zest and sprigs of fresh mint. Serve immediately.

THE BIG APPLE

★ ★ ★ ★ ★

The way to eat this fruity extravaganza is warm with a generous helping of whipped cream.

SERVES 2

2 dessert apples, peeled and chopped

25 g/1 oz caster sugar

pinch of ground cinnamon

15 g/½ oz butter or margarine, plus extra for spreading

1 cinnamon and raisin bagel

whipped cream, to serve

METHOD

Place the chopped apple, sugar, ground cinnamon and butter in a saucepan with 60–75 ml/4–5 tbsp water. Bring the apple mixture to the boil, then simmer for about 5 minutes, until the apple is tender. Drain and cool until warm.

Meanwhile, cut the bagel in half horizontally and pull out the bagel dough from the middle of each half to make a hollow ring.

Butter the inside of the bagel rings, then place in a very low oven to warm through.

Spoon the apple mixture into the warmed, hollowed out bagels and serve with a dollop of whipped cream.

BLACK FOREST BAGEL

★ ★ ★ ★ ★

A luxurious combination of black cherries and cream coated in a velvety smooth, cherry sauce.

SERVES 2

2 cinnamon and raisin bagels

60 ml/4 tbsp kirsch liqueur

400 g/14 oz can black cherries in syrup, drained, syrup reserved

300 ml/½ pint double cream

2 tbsp sifted icing sugar

few drops of vanilla essence

1 tbsp arrowroot

fresh mint sprigs, to decorate

METHOD

Slice a thin layer off the top of each bagel, then hollow it out with your fingers, pulling out the dough from the centre of the bagel.

Sprinkle about 15 ml/1 tbsp of the kirsch over the insides of each bagel. Place all but a few of the cherries in the hollowed bagels.

Put the cream in a mixing bowl and add the icing sugar and vanilla essence. Whisk, using an electric hand mixer, until the cream holds soft peaks. Divide the cream mixture between the bagels, piling it up quite high.

Put about 150 ml/¼ pint of the reserved cherry syrup in a small saucepan. In a small bowl, mix the arrowroot with enough of the cherry syrup to make a smooth paste. Heat the syrup until boiling. Stir in the arrowroot mixture and return to the boil, stirring continuously, until shiny and thickened. Cool slightly.

Arrange the reserved cherries on the cream on each bagel, then pour over the warm sauce and serve immediately, decorated with sprigs of fresh mint.

Black Forest Bagel

A TRIFLE BAGEL

★ ★ ★ ★ ★

*A perfect treat for a Sunday lunchtime pudding for all the family.
Multiply the quantities of ingredients, depending on how many Trifle
Bagels you'll need.*

SERVES 2

1 cinnamon and raisin bagel

200 g/7 oz can raspberries in syrup, drained

90–100 ml/6–7 tbsp made custard

150 ml/¼ pint double cream

coloured hundreds and thousands, to decorate

METHOD

Cut the bagel in half horizontally and scoop out the dough from the middle, using your fingers, to make a hollow channel.

Put the bagel halves on individual serving plates and divide all but a few of the raspberries between them. Reserve the remainder. Press the raspberries down gently in the bagel bases, then spoon the custard on top.

Put the cream in a mixing bowl and whisk with an electric hand mixer until it holds soft peaks. Divide the cream between the bagels, then scatter over the reserved raspberries. Sprinkle with hundreds and thousands, then serve immediately.

TROPICAL DREAM

★ ★ ★ ★ ★

*This bagel is colourful and fruity. You can make use of whatever
tropical fruits you can find and mix them with other tiny soft fruits.*

SERVES 2

1 cinnamon and raisin bagel

150 ml/¼ pint double cream

1 tbsp icing sugar

few drops of vanilla essence

225 g/8 oz mixed tropical fruits, such as star fruit, papaya, kiwi and other soft fruits

75–90 ml/5–6 tbsp tropical fruit juice drink

2 tbsp arrowroot

tiny lemon geranium sprigs, to decorate

METHOD

Cut the bagel in half horizontally and toast. Place each bagel half on an individual serving plate.

Put the cream in a mixing bowl with the icing sugar and vanilla essence. Whisk with an electric hand mixer until it holds soft peaks.

Divide the cream mixture between the bagel halves and spread out evenly. Arrange the fruits on top.

Mix enough of the tropical fruit juice drink with the arrowroot in a small bowl to make a smooth paste. Heat the remaining juice in a saucepan until boiling. Stir in the arrowroot paste and bring the sauce back to the boil, stirring continuously, until thickened, smooth and shiny. Cool slightly.

Drizzle the sauce over the bagel halves. Decorate with tiny sprigs of lemon geranium, to serve.

Tropical Dream

PECAN TOPPERS

★ ★ ★ ★ ★

These nutty bagels are deliciously sweet and sticky.

SERVES 2

1 cinnamon and raisin bagel

butter or margarine, for spreading

60–75 ml/4–5 tbsp butterscotch sauce

75 g/3 oz shelled pecan nuts, chopped

METHOD

Cut the bagel in half horizontally and butter the cut surfaces. Lightly toast, until golden.

Place the butterscotch sauce in a bowl and stir in the chopped pecan nuts. Divide the pecan mixture between the bagels and spread evenly. Serve immediately.

STRAWBERRY FAYRE

★ ★ ★ ★ ★

This delightful summertime extravaganza combines ice-cream with whipped cream, fresh strawberries and a freshly baked, warm cinnamon bagel.

SERVES 2

2 cinnamon and raisin bagels

150 ml/¼ pint double cream

2 tbsp icing sugar, sifted

few drops of vanilla essence

100 g/4 oz fresh strawberries, hulled and sliced

2 large scoops of luxury strawberry ice-cream

30–45 ml/2–3 tbsp strawberry sauce

strawberries, sifted icing sugar and fresh mint sprigs, to decorate

METHOD

Cut a "V" shape out of the centre of each bagel. Discard the "V" shape, slice the bagels in half and place the bagel bases in a low oven to warm.

Meanwhile, put the cream in a mixing bowl with the icing sugar and vanilla essence. Whisk, using an electric hand mixer, until the cream holds soft peaks.

Place the bagel bases on individual serving plates and divide the whipped cream mixture between them. Arrange the sliced strawberries on top.

Put a scoop of ice-cream on top of the strawberries, then drizzle with strawberry sauce. Decorate with a strawberry, sifted icing sugar and sprigs of fresh mint.

INDEX

★ ★ ★ ★ ★